I0814245

RUNNING THE SHOW

The Evolving Roles of Sports Owners

By Luke Hanlon

SportsZone

An Imprint of Abdo Publishing
abdobooks.com

abdobooks.com

Published by Abdo Publishing, a division of ABDO, PO Box 398166, Minneapolis, Minnesota 55439. Copyright © 2026 by Abdo Consulting Group, Inc. International copyrights reserved in all countries. No part of this book may be reproduced in any form without written permission from the publisher. SportsZone™ is a trademark and logo of Abdo Publishing.

Printed in the United States of America, North Mankato, Minnesota.
102025
012026

Cover Photo: Katelyn Mulcahy/Getty Images Sport/Getty Images
Interior Photos: Bruce Bennett/Getty Images Sport/Getty Images, 1, 8; Brace Hemmelgarn/Minnesota Twins/Getty Images Sport/Getty Images, 3, 34–35; Aaron Ontiveroz/Denver Post/Getty Images, 4–5; Matthew Stockman/Getty Images Sport/Getty Images, 6–7; Catherine Ivill/Getty Images Sport/Getty Images, 10; Michael B. Thomas/Getty Images Sport/Getty Images, 12; Stock Montage/Archive Photos/Getty Images, 14–15; Bettmann/Getty Images, 17; Ronald Martinez/Getty Images Sport/Getty Images, 18; Al Gretz/Keystone View Company/Archive Photos/Getty Images, 20; Harry How/Getty Images Sport/Getty Images, 20–21, 45; Charles Krupa/AP Images, 22; Sean M. Haffey/Getty Images Sport/Getty Images, 24–25, 30, 47; Austin McAfee/Icon Sportswire/Getty Images, 26–27; Stephen Dunn/Allsport/Hulton Archive/Getty Images, 28; Ethan Miller/Getty Images Sport/Getty Images, 33; Thomas A. Ferrara/Newsday RM/Newsday LLC/Getty Images, 37; Steve Heap/Shutterstock Images, 39; Jeff Gross/Getty Images Sport/Getty Images, 40; Lindsey Wasson/AP Images, 42–43

Editor: Christa Kelly
Series Designer: Maggie Villaume

Library of Congress Control Number: 2025939200

Publisher's Cataloging-in-Publication Data

Names: Hanlon, Luke, author.
Title: Running the show: the evolving roles of sports owners / by Luke Hanlon
Description: Minneapolis, Minnesota: Abdo Publishing, 2026 | Series: The business of sports | Includes online resources and index.
Identifiers: ISBN 9781098298272 (lib. bdg.) | ISBN 9798384932079 (ebook)
Subjects: LCSH: Sports--Juvenile literature. | Sports team owners--Juvenile literature. | Sports promoters--Juvenile literature. | Sports general managers--Juvenile literature. | Sports executives--Juvenile literature. | Sports in popular culture--Juvenile literature.
Classification: DDC 796.023--dc23

TABLE OF CONTENTS

WU
Western Union
DENVER
5
MIAMI
2

CHAPTER ONE

SETTING THE STANDARD

Fans in Denver's Ball Arena eagerly watched the clock wind down. The Nuggets led the Miami Heat 94–89 in Game 5 of the 2023 National Basketball Association (NBA) Finals. With 12 seconds left, Miami guard Kyle Lowry launched a three-pointer. The shot clanked off the rim. Nuggets guard Kentavious Caldwell-Pope rebounded the miss and dribbled out the clock. The sold-out crowd erupted as the Nuggets clinched their first NBA championship.

The Nuggets gathered on the court in celebration. Adam Silver, the NBA commissioner, joined them to present the Larry O'Brien Trophy. But as is tradition in most American sports, Silver first handed the trophy to the team's owner, Stan Kroenke. "It means a lot to us to get this done, and the fans, we couldn't have done it without

Kentavious Caldwell-Pope averaged 7.4 points per game in the 2023 NBA finals.

them," Kroenke said. Nuggets fans had waited 47 years for their team to win the NBA title. Meanwhile, Kroenke had just won his fourth championship in less than two years.

Becoming an Owner

Many fans view professional sports as a fun pastime. But leagues such as the NBA are big businesses. The NBA is made up of 30 teams. Each team is worth billions of dollars. And each one is owned and operated independently. Naturally, a team's athletes attract most of the attention. But it's the team's owner who sets the foundation for the entire operation.

Sports owners oversee every aspect of the teams they control. This means they have a range of responsibilities. Owners hire the executives who run their teams. Owners determine how much money to spend on rosters and facilities. They also ensure their teams are bringing in enough money. An effective owner can be the difference between a successful team and a flop.

Stan Kroenke, *right*, helped the Denver Nuggets win the team's first NBA Finals appearance.

22-23 NBA
Champions

Kroenke has always been passionate about sports.

Born and raised in Missouri, Kroenke made billions of dollars in real estate. In the 1990s, he tried to bring a National Football League (NFL) expansion team to St. Louis. However, he couldn't convince the league to add a new team. Instead, he reached out to Georgia Frontiere.

Frontiere's husband, businessman Carroll Rosenbloom, had owned the Los Angeles Rams. When he died in 1979, Frontiere took over and became the NFL's first female owner. By the 1990s, however, the team was losing money. Knowing Frontiere was originally from St. Louis, Kroenke approached her about moving the Rams to her hometown. In 1995, she agreed to sell him a 30 percent stake in the team for $60 million. That fall, the Rams played their first game in Missouri. In 2000, following the team's fifth season in the new city, the Rams won the Super Bowl.

Adding Teams

Soon after buying into the Rams, Kroenke began thinking bigger. In 1999, he started Kroenke Sports & Entertainment (KSE). Using his new company, Kroenke began building a sports empire.

In 2000, KSE bought the Denver Nuggets basketball team, the Colorado Avalanche hockey team, and the arena both teams played in. The following year, KSE bought the Colorado Mammoth of the National Lacrosse League (NLL). KSE took control of the Colorado Rapids, a Major League Soccer team, in 2003. Then, in 2004, Kroenke launched Altitude Sports and Entertainment, a local TV channel that aired all of Kroenke's Colorado teams' games. A few years later, Kroenke bought part of the Arsenal FC, one of the most popular soccer teams in England.

In 2020, Arsenal won its fourth Football Association Challenge Cup with Kroenke as an owner.

Kroenke's investments made him a prominent figure in American sports. Then he got his biggest opportunity yet. When Frontiere died in 2008, she passed her ownership stake on to her children. Two years later, they sold the rest of the team to Kroenke for $750 million. Kroenke was now the Rams' majority owner. He finally controlled the team.

A Sports Titan

Kroenke's record as an owner has been mixed. The Rams had enjoyed success early in Kroenke's time as a minority owner. And the Avalanche won a Stanley Cup title in Kroenke's first season. But he has also faced difficulties and criticism. Arsenal fans had long been skeptical of the American owner. Many called for him to sell the team after KSE briefly supported an effort to create a European Super League.

Back in Colorado, KSE's Altitude TV channel had created a new revenue stream for the teams. However, KSE disagreed with cable providers about how much they should pay for the channel. This dispute caused Avalanche and Nuggets games to be unavailable to many TV viewers for years. Some fans were upset. It didn't help that Kroenke rarely made public appearances. Fans nicknamed him Silent Stan.

Kroenke's most controversial move happened in St. Louis. By the 2010s, the Rams were seeking a new stadium. The city of St. Louis proposed plans to help build one. But Kroenke said he needed more public money. He also said the city didn't have enough people to support an NFL team. In 2016, he moved the Rams back to Los Angeles.

BENDING THE RULES

Sports leagues want their owners to be dedicated to their teams and their cities. One way the NFL ensures its owners' loyalty is by barring owners from running pro teams in other NFL cities. Since the NFL's Broncos play in Denver, Stan Kroenke had to give up control of the Nuggets and the Avalanche when he bought the Rams. Instead of selling the teams, Kroenke gave full control of them to his son Josh.

Many fans protested the decision to move the Rams out of St. Louis.

Fans in St. Louis were furious. The city itself even sued Kroenke for unlawfully moving the team. But Kroenke had a vision. He thought he'd be more successful back in Los Angeles. Although Kroenke didn't receive any public money as had been offered in St. Louis, he invested $5 billion to build SoFi Stadium in the suburb of Inglewood, California. When it opened in 2020, the stadium was immediately one of the nation's premier venues.

Kroenke had more changes to make. The Rams had gone 12 seasons without a winning record in St. Louis. Kroenke decided it was time for a new coach. In 2017, Kroenke hired 30-year-old Sean McVay, one of the brightest coaching stars in the NFL. The team's fortunes quickly changed. McVay led the Rams to the Super Bowl in 2018 after his second season.

On February 13, 2022, the team returned to the Super Bowl. This time it happened to be taking place in SoFi Stadium. With Kroenke looking on from his new state-of-the-art stadium, his team beat the Cincinnati Bengals 23–20.

The win marked a high point in Kroenke's long run as a sports owner. And KSE's success was only just beginning. Four months after the Super Bowl, the Mammoth won the NLL championship. Just over a week later, the Avalanche won the Stanley Cup. Then in June 2023, the Nuggets won the team's first NBA title. In just three decades, Kroenke had set a new standard for sports owners.

Today, the roles of sports owners are increasingly important. Their guidance can set teams up for successful, lucrative seasons. But bad decisions can bankrupt teams and drive away fans. For sports owners, the industry is more than just a game. It's a job.

CHAPTER TWO

HUMBLE BEGINNINGS

Chicago businessman William Hulbert bought a small share of the Chicago White Stockings, now known as the Chicago Cubs, in 1870. By 1875, he'd taken over as the team's president. At the time, baseball teams folded frequently. And professional leagues didn't last more than a few years. One pro league allowed any team to enter for a $10 fee. So, in February 1876, Hulbert convinced seven other team owners to form the National League (NL). Hulbert didn't allow any other teams to join the league. He hoped that this would keep it running for years.

The NL consisted of teams in the Northeast and Midwest. Team owners were often local businessmen who spent most of their money buying teams. Sometimes, multiple partners would invest in a team together.

The Chicago White Stockings were Chicago's first professional baseball team.

Team owners were generally heavily involved in the operations of their teams. They decided where their teams played games and how much to charge for tickets. And they often built their teams' rosters themselves.

COMMISSIONERS

Each major professional sports league in the United States has a commissioner. A commissioner oversees every aspect of a league. That includes negotiating media deals, enforcing league rules, promoting the league, and much more. Each league's owners vote to elect their commissioners. So the commissioners often work in the owners' best interest.

Expenses

Though owners can earn a lot of money from sports teams, it is also a costly business. Even joining a league can cost millions. But that wasn't always the case.

In 1920, George Halas paid a $100 fee for the Decatur Staleys, now the NFL's Chicago Bears. A former pro baseball player, Halas wasn't a wealthy man. The Chicago native bought the team because he loved sports and wanted to see a local team thrive. He ended up playing for, coaching, and owning the Bears.

However, in the following decades, sports ownership became much more expensive. The Dallas Cowboys started as an NFL expansion team in 1960. The Minnesota Vikings joined the league a year later. The owners of the teams had to each pay the league $1 million to join the NFL. And the owners

The Chicago Bears won the NFL Championship six times with George Halas, *center*, as owner.

were much different from Halas. Clint Murchison Sr. was one of the richest oilmen in Texas when he paid $1 million for the Cowboys. In Minnesota, five different local businessmen pooled their money together to buy into the NFL.

Bob McNair owned the Houston Texans until his death in 2018.

The NFL expanded again in 2002 when the Houston Texans joined the league. Three years earlier, Bob McNair sold his power generator company for $1.5 billion. That provided him with more than enough money to pay the $700 million expansion fee for the Texans.

But even those who have the money might not be able to buy a team. In the NFL, owners can vote on if they want to allow a new owner into the league. Three-fourths of the owners need to approve the sale. Then, the buyer needs to cover at least 30 percent of the team's value. In 2024, the Cincinnati Bengals were the lowest-valued NFL team at $5.25 billion. If a new owner wanted to buy them, they'd need to have at least $1.58 billion.

Making Money

Buying a team is expensive. But it can also be a good investment. Sports owners make money from broadcast rights, merchandise, and more.

Sports owners have been making money off sports for more than 100 years. In the early days of pro baseball, owners made most of their money on game days. This meant that attracting fans was a key part of owning a team. In the late 1800s, Chris von der Ahe owned baseball's St. Louis Browns. He built an amusement park just beyond the outfield wall at the team's stadium to attract more fans to games.

In the 1920s, radio presented a new way for sports owners to make money. Radio stations would pay teams for the rights to broadcast their games over the air. But many owners didn't want their games on the radio. They believed that would encourage fans to stay home instead of going to the ballpark to watch games. However, owners soon realized radio broadcasts helped them gain fans. The radio broadcasts provided advertising for teams.

The St. Louis Browns were part of the American Association. The team was later renamed the St. Louis Cardinals.

In the mid-1940s, television created another way for sports owners to make money. By 1955, every Major League Baseball (MLB) team broadcast some of its games locally on TV. But no league embraced television more than the NFL.

In 1960, Pete Rozelle became the commissioner of the NFL. One year later, he signed a national TV contract for the league. Under the new deal, the league split the broadcasting fee evenly among all the team owners. This is called revenue sharing. Each team received $332,000 each year from the contract.

Media rights deals have continued to grow since the 2000s, sharply increasing the valuation of sports teams. From 2014 to 2024, all major American sports teams rose in value. The average NBA team value increased by 499 percent. The NFL is even more lucrative. The league makes billions of dollars each season. In 2023, each team made $400 million from revenue sharing.

The high price of sports teams has shrunk the list of potential owners. The days of local investors buying major professional teams are gone. Billionaires or groups of wealthy investors are the main purchasers of major sports teams today. In 2014, former Microsoft chief executive officer (CEO) Steve Ballmer bought the NBA's

The 2023–24 NBA season marked the Los Angeles Clippers' tenth winning season under owner Steve Ballmer.

Los Angeles Clippers for $2 billion. The Clippers have turned a profit most years since Ballmer has owned the team. But even if they don't, Ballmer can make money by selling the team. In 2025, the Clippers were worth an estimated $5.4 billion.

Though selling a team can net billions of dollars, few owners do. They make long-term profits by keeping their teams. When owners die, their teams are often passed down to their children. By 2025, more than a dozen of the NFL's 32 teams were run by the child or grandchild of a former owner. And eight of those owners inherited the franchise from the team's founder. That includes the Bears, which has stayed in the Halas family since 1920.

The Boston Celtics won the 2024 NBA Championships 4–1.

CASE STUDY

SOARING PRICES

The Boston Celtics are one of the three original NBA teams that still exist. The team's long history of winning began in 1956 when it drafted Bill Russell. The talented center led the Celtics to 11 championships in 13 years.

Boston remained one of the NBA's top teams for decades. In 2002, Boston Basketball Partners bought the Celtics for $360 million. Co-owners Wyc Grousbeck and Steve Pagliuca ran the team and kept it successful. With the duo in charge, the Celtics won the NBA title in 2008 and 2024, bringing Boston to 18 championships. That is more than any other NBA team.

In the decades since Grousbeck and Pagliuca bought the team, the NBA rose in popularity. In 2024, the NBA announced a new national media deal worth $6.9 billion per year. Starting in the 2025–26 season, each team would receive $230 million each year from the deal.

After winning the 2024 title, Grousbeck and Pagliuca decided to put the team up for sale. With the new media deal in place, potential buyers lined up to put in an offer for the Celtics. A group led by tech billionaire Bill Chisholm bought the team for $6.1 billion in 2025. At the time of the sale, it was the most expensive purchase of a North American sports team in history.

bibigo
LAKERS
77

CHAPTER THREE

RUNNING A TEAM

NBA icon Luka Dončić walked off the court after a game against the Dallas Mavericks. He had scored 45 points for the Los Angeles Lakers. But the fans in Dallas gave him a massive standing ovation.

Two months before, Dallas general manager (GM) Nico Harrison traded Dončić to Los Angeles. At only 25, Dončić was one of the best players in the league. During the 2024 playoffs, the superstar guard led the Mavericks to the NBA Finals. Despite losing the series, the Mavericks' future looked bright with Dončić leading the way.

When Dallas fans learned that Dončić was being traded, they were infuriated. Before Dallas's first home game after the move, hundreds of fans gathered outside the team's arena to protest

Luka Dončić, *left*, played for the Dallas Mavericks for seven seasons before being traded to the Los Angeles Lakers.

the trade. Many of them wore Dončić jerseys. Some held signs that read "Fire Nico."

Harrison was the person who had come up with the idea for the deal. But he was not the only one affected by the protests. Mavericks owner Patrick Dumont was feeling the heat from angry fans. He was booed at home games. The situation felt like a nightmare.

Dumont had become co-owner of the team in 2023. Before that, he had been a businessman. He had always trusted the employees he hired. He used the same philosophy running the Mavericks. He had trusted in Harrison's basketball experience when he approved the controversial trade. But that decision had come back to bite him.

Tough Decisions

Most sports owners run their teams like Dumont. They aren't involved in the day-to-day management of their teams. They hire people to take on those responsibilities. Much of the work is done by a GM. GMs build their teams' rosters. They draft and

Fans were enraged that Dončić was traded.

LUKA MAGIC
WILL NEVER DIE
IN DALLAS
FIRE NICO
SELL THE TEA
AWA
INVESTIGAT
INVESTIGA
INVESTIGAT
INVESTIGATE
WE'LL MISS YO
LUKA
THANKS FOR THE MAGIC
LUKA 7
IS THE
CULTU
DONČIĆ
DALLAS

trade players. They sign free agents. GMs often hire coaches too. Owners may make the final calls, but most largely trust their GMs to manage their teams. This can lead to problems when GMs make unpopular decisions. At the end of the day, fans may blame the owners. And angry fans might stop spending money on their favorite teams.

However, not all owners give up control of their teams. Businessman Jerry Jones bought the NFL's Dallas Cowboys in 1989. Along with being the Cowboys' owner, he decided to serve as the team's GM.

Tom Landry had coached the team since its first season in 1960 and led Dallas to two Super Bowl wins. So fans were

Jerry Jones bought the Dallas Cowboys for $150 million.

shocked when Jones decided to fire Landry on the same day he bought the team. Right away, Jones showed he wasn't afraid to make bold decisions.

Initially, Jones's aggressive approach paid off. In the early 1990s, the Cowboys won three Super Bowls in a four-year span. However, since 1996, the Cowboys have won only five playoff games. Many Dallas fans blame Jones for the team's lack of success. His style of running all aspects of a team is much different from other owners who rely on experienced football professionals to put together a roster.

Buying a Roster

One of the main decisions an owner must make is how much money they want to spend on their team. Better players often cost more money. Teams that spend more money on players typically have more success.

In no league does payroll play a bigger role in determining the winner than in MLB. Unlike most American professional leagues, MLB doesn't have a hard salary cap. This means there's no limit to the amount teams can spend on their rosters.

In 2024, the New York Mets, New York Yankees, and Los Angeles Dodgers had the three most expensive rosters in the league. All three teams made it to the semifinals of the playoffs. The Dodgers then won the World Series.

Shohei Ohtani played for the Los Angeles Angels for six seasons before being traded to the Los Angeles Dodgers.

Many attributed the Dodgers' success to their most expensive player. In 2023, the team signed Shohei Ohtani to a 10-year, $700-million contract. The Japanese superstar had already won multiple Most Valuable Player (MVP) Awards with the crosstown Los Angeles Angels. He added another MVP in his first year with the Dodgers. And he helped a roster already loaded with talent win the World Series.

Some owners try to save money by not spending much on their rosters. But this can backfire. In 2005, John Fisher bought the Oakland Athletics (A's) for $180 million. In the following years, Fisher traded away some of the team's best players. This allowed him to spend less on his team's roster. In 2024, the A's had the lowest payroll in the league by more than $20 million.

Though Fisher was spending less money, he was also making less. Without the A's best players, the team struggled. Fans didn't want to root for a losing team. Many stopped attending games. This cost Fisher a great deal of money.

Attracting Players

Part of building rosters is attracting free agents. Owners play big roles in this. The easiest way to attract a free agent is by offering them more money than other teams. But due to salary caps, that isn't always possible. So owners have to get creative with their spending.

While leagues have caps on salaries, they don't limit the amount of money teams can spend on other kinds of benefits. Teams can spend as much as they want on coaching and training staff. Having better trainers can also help keep players healthy, which pays off in dividends.

Owners can also spend money to upgrade their practice facilities. No league has a bigger gap in the quality of team facilities than the Women's National Basketball Association (WNBA). Some teams use their own arenas

REPORT CARDS

The NFL Players Association has its players grade their teams each season. Players grade their teams' facilities, their teams' training and coaching staff, how the team treats their families, and more. Every owner receives a grade as well. This report card helps free agents learn about a team's pros and cons. It also holds owners accountable if they aren't supporting their players.

to practice. Others share a facility with NBA teams. Still other teams practice in college gyms.

After buying the WNBA's Las Vegas Aces in 2021, Mark Davis heavily invested in his new team. Davis hired a new coach, Becky Hammon, and paid her a league-high $1 million per year. Hammon led the Aces to their first WNBA championship in 2022.

A year later, the Aces spent $40 million to build the first practice facility exclusively for a WNBA team. Before the 2023 season, star free agent Candace Parker signed with the Aces. She said the practice facility affected her decision. With Parker's help, the Aces repeated as champions.

Changing the Rules

In most American professional sports leagues, owners get the chance to change the rules of their leagues. Any owner in a league can propose a rule change. The rest of the league's owners then vote on whether to make the change. The proposed changes don't have to just be about the rules of

In 2023, the Las Vegas Aces won the WNBA championship 3–1 against the New York Liberty.

the game. Owners can try to adjust rules about anything the league oversees.

Each league has different requirements for changing rules. In the NFL, at least 75 percent of the league's owners need to agree to change a rule. In 2025, the owner of the Detroit Lions proposed a rule change. She no longer wanted defensive penalties to result in an automatic first down for the offense. The NFL owners rejected that change.

The owner of the Philadelphia Eagles successfully changed a rule. He proposed using the same overtime rules for the regular season and playoffs. The rest of the owners agreed that this was a good idea.

CHAPTER FOUR

RUNNING A BUSINESS

Carlos Santana stepped up to the plate. The first baseman had a chance to be a hero for the Minnesota Twins. Santana's team was tied 6–6 with the Tampa Bay Rays in the bottom of the ninth inning in a June 2024 game.

On the third pitch of his at-bat, Santana slapped the ball just past Tampa Bay's second baseman. Minnesota's Manuel Margot raced from second base all the way home. The crowd in Minnesota roared as Santana's walk-off hit secured the Twins' seventh win in a row.

This moment wasn't as exciting for fans who were not at the stadium. That's because many of them couldn't watch the game. Before the 2024 season, Minnesota's owner, Jim Pohlad, agreed to a local TV deal with Bally Sports North (BSN). The channel appeared on many cable packages

Carlos Santana joined the Minnesota Twins in 2024.

in Minnesota. But most fans who used streaming platforms didn't have access to the network.

BSN was also on the verge of bankruptcy. The channel couldn't pay the Twins as much as it had the previous season. This meant the Twins had less money to spend on payroll. Pohlad cut the team's pay by more than $35 million. After winning a playoff series in 2023, the Twins missed the postseason altogether in 2024. It was a clear example of how an owner's decisions can affect a team's success.

Making a Deal

Building a competitive team is only part of an owner's job. An owner must also run a successful business. There are many deals and decisions owners must make to keep their teams successful. And their choices impact much more than just their own financial gains or losses.

Media deals are among the most important deals owners negotiate. Local media deals often produce a large chunk of a team's profit. Losing these deals can mean losing players and games.

Some professional teams don't have to deal with outside networks broadcasting their games. That's because they run their own local networks. In 2002, the New York Yankees' owner, George Steinbrenner, created the

In 2022, viewers watched more than 10 billion minutes of New York Yankees games on the YES Network and app.

Yankees Entertainment & Sports (YES) Network. That gave him full control over the team's broadcasts. And the network has made the team a lot of money over the years.

The Yankees can sell their broadcasting rights directly to fans. The team charged fans $239.99 to get access to all their local broadcasts in 2023. This adds up. The previous season, the Yankees made $143 million from broadcasting. Following the success of the YES Network, dozens of sports teams have created their own channels as well.

Funding a Stadium

One of the largest investments a sports owner can make is in their team's stadium. When an owner decides they want a new stadium, they first have to decide how to pay for it. Some owners pay for stadiums themselves. This gives them total control over how the stadium is used.

In 2002, Robert Kraft spent $325 million to build a new stadium for his NFL team, the New England Patriots. In addition to Patriots games, the stadium regularly hosts other events, such as concerts and international soccer games. Kraft makes money from the stadium hosting these events. He even makes money from the events' concessions.

Kraft is a rare example, though. The Patriots are one of five NFL teams that own their own stadium. That's because building a stadium is expensive. Since 2005, every new NFL stadium has cost at least $1 billion. To help get stadiums built, owners often rely on money from local taxpayers.

The Tennessee Titans have an agreement with the city to have a stadium there until 2039. Instead of spending more than $1 billion of public money on upgrading their current stadium, the Titans began planning to build a new one. In 2023, they approved a plan for a new stadium that would cost $2.1 billion. Taxpayers will cover $1.26 billion of that bill. That's the most public funding ever provided for an American sports stadium.

Economists argue that taxpayers rarely get good value when they pay for sports stadiums. One reason is that the public doesn't get access to the stadium like they would a public park or sports field. And most of the money made from events at the stadium goes back to the team, not the local economy.

However, Nashville mayor John Cooper said the new Titans stadium would benefit the city. Titans owner Amy Adams Strunk said the new stadium would ensure the Titans stayed in Nashville for decades to come. That proved to be enough for Nashville's city council to approve the plans for the new venue.

Making sure a team remains in a city is a big reason taxpayers will fork out cash for a stadium. No matter the cost, fans want to keep the connection they have with their local teams. That argument doesn't always work, though.

Throughout the early 2010s, San Diego Chargers owner Dean Spanos tried to get a new stadium built in the city.

The Tennessee Titans' new stadium was built to replace the old Nissan Stadium.

Before the San Diego Chargers moved to Los Angeles, they played at Qualcomm Stadium.

To raise money, the city proposed raising hotel fees to help fund the stadium. People in San Diego voted against that. Meanwhile, the city council wouldn't agree to use tax dollars for the stadium.

With no way to build a stadium in San Diego, Spanos moved the team to Los Angeles in 2017. He had to pay a $550 million relocation fee. And the Chargers still didn't have their own stadium in Los Angeles. They play in SoFi Stadium, which the

Los Angeles Rams own. The lack of connection with San Diego impacts the team as well. At many of the Chargers' home games, there are more away fans than Chargers fans.

VALUE MENU

Going to a sporting event can be expensive. In 2024, the average cost for a family of four to go to an NFL game was $631. Atlanta Falcons owner Arthur Blank has tried to make it less costly for families to attend games. When the Falcons moved to a new stadium in 2017, Blank reduced concession prices. The Falcons had the cheapest concessions in the NFL by far. Yet the team ended up making more money from sales than they did at their old stadium.

Game Day

Keeping a stadium filled is an important part of owning a sports team. Selling season tickets is the easiest way to do that. They provide fans with tickets to every home game in a year. That brings in consistent revenue for the team. Plus, having fans at games leads to other opportunities for them to spend money. Sales from parking, concessions, team merchandise, and more all help a team's business.

Joe Lacob and Peter Gruber are masters at filling stadiums. Lacob and Gruber own the NBA's Golden State Warriors. Throughout the late 2010s, the Warriors were one of the most successful teams in the NBA.

In 2023, Lacob and Gruber paid a $50 million expansion fee to get a WNBA team. They named the team the

Golden State Valkyries. Lacob and Gruber hired Jess Smith to run the Valkyries. She led the charge in selling season tickets before the team's first season. By March 25, the Valkyries became the first WNBA team to sell more than 10,000 season tickets.

The Valkyries' first game was on May 16, 2025. Thanks to years of promotion before the team ever took to the court, the stadium was packed. More than 18,000 fans gathered to witness the team's first game. In the months that followed, the Valkyries continued to play in front of packed houses during each home game. The team's success started with the hard work of the owners.

In 2023, Angel City FC made it to the NWSL quarterfinals.

CASE STUDY

COMMUNITY TEAM

During the 2019 Women's World Cup, investor Kara Nortman, businesswoman Julie Uhrman, and actress Natalie Portman came up with an idea. Inspired by the connection fans had with their national teams, they decided to start their own soccer team. A year later, Angel City FC was born.

The three founders wanted their women's soccer team to help its community in Los Angeles. So the team gives 10 percent of its profit made from sponsors back to the city. The new team attracted many famous investors. Tennis icons Billie Jean King and Serena Williams bought into the team. So did 13 former US women's soccer national team players. Actresses such as America Ferrera invested in the team, too.

In 2022, Angel City FC played its first season in the National Women's Soccer League (NWSL). By 2023, the team had made the most revenue of any women's sports team in the world. Fans connected with the team right away. Angel City FC led the NWSL in attendance in 2023.

In 2024, investors Willow Bay and Bob Iger bought a majority share in Angel City FC. The deal valued the club at $250 million. That made Angel City FC the most valuable women's sports team in the world.

TIMELINE

1876

William Hulbert, the owner of the Chicago White Stockings, creates the NL.

1961

The NFL agrees to a national TV deal and splits the revenue with NFL team owners.

1989

Jerry Jones buys the Dallas Cowboys and fires longtime head coach Tom Landry.

1999

Stan Kroenke founds KSE, a company that will go on to manage his sports teams.

2002

Robert Kraft pays $325 million to fully fund a new stadium for the New England Patriots.

2014

Steve Ballmer buys the Los Angeles Clippers for $2 billion.

2016

More than 20 years after bringing the Rams to St. Louis, Stan Kroenke moves the Rams back to Los Angeles.

2020

Kara Nortman, Julie Uhrman, and Natalie Portman create Angel City FC.

2023

The Las Vegas Aces open the first practice facility fully dedicated to a WNBA team.

2024

John Fisher moves the A's out of Oakland after 57 years in the city.

2025

A group led by Bill Chisholm buys the Boston Celtics for $6.1 billion, the highest price paid for a North American sports team.

GLOSSARY

bankrupt
To cause a business to be unable to pay a debt, often leading it to close.

concessions
Food and drinks sold at a sporting event.

contract
A financial agreement.

draft
To add a new player to a team.

expansion team
A new team that is added to an existing league.

fold
To go out of business.

franchise
A sports organization, including the top-level team and all minor league affiliates.

free agent
A player who is not signed to a team.

general manager
An executive who runs a team and is responsible for finding and signing players.

icon
Someone who is well known.

merchandise
Goods to be bought and sold.

revenue
The amount of money a company makes.

roster
A list of players who make up a team.

salary cap
A limit on the amount of money that teams can pay players.

share
A part of a company that can be owned.

MORE INFORMATION

BOOKS

Hanlon, Luke. *Broadcast Rights: The Future of TV and Streaming*. Abdo, 2026.

Illustrated Sports Encyclopedia. DK, 2023.

Schad, Tom. *Managing the Money: Athlete Contracts and Salary Caps*. Abdo, 2026.

ONLINE RESOURCES

To learn more about sports owners, please visit **abdobooklinks.com** or scan this QR code. These links are routinely monitored and updated to provide the most current information available.

INDEX

ABOUT THE AUTHOR

Luke Hanlon is a sportswriter and editor who lives in Minneapolis, Minnesota. He's written dozens of nonfiction sports books for kids and spends a lot of his free time watching his favorite Minnesota sports teams.